paktya

PROVINCIAL HANDBOOK / A Guide to the People and the Province

Kurram Agency
(FATA Pakistan)

Sapari

Dand
Wa
Patan

Chamkani

Zazi Aryoub

Share
Now

Zazi

Jani Khel

Ahmad Khel

Ahmad Khel

Lija Mangal

Lija Mangal

Jani Khel

Mirzaka

Mirzaka

Sayed Karam

Waza
Zadran

Sayed Karam

Gardez

Shwak

Waza

Khost

Sayed Karam

Waza

Shwak

Gerda Serai

Ahmad
Abad

Ahmad
Abad

Shwak

Gerda Serai

Gerda Serai

Logar

Zormat

Gardez

Zormat

Zormat

Paktya

Roads
District Border
River
Provincial Center
City

HIGHER ELEVATION

LOWER ELEVATION

Ghazni

Paktika

Table of Contents

List of Tables and Maps

Acronyms and Key Terms

ABP	Afghan Border Police
ADT	Agribusiness Development Team
ANA	Afghan National Army
ANBP	Afghan National Border Police
ANDS	Afghan National Development Strategy
ANP	Afghan National Police
ANSF	Afghan National Security Forces
Arbakai	A volunteer, tribal police force which follows a strict ethical code
AWCC	Afghan Wireless Communication Company
BEFA	Basic Education for Afghanistan
BPHS	Basic Package of Health Services
CA	Civil Affairs
CDCs	Community Development Councils
CERP	Commander's Emergency Response Program
CHC	Comprehensive Health Centers
COIN	Counter Insurgency
CSO	Central Statistics Office
DDS	District Development Shuras
DIAG	Disbandment of Illegal Armed Groups
DoS	US Department of State
DST	District Support Team
FATA	Federally Administered Tribal Areas
GIRoA	Government of the Islamic Republic of Afghanistan
HIG or HIH	Hezb-e Islami Gulbuddin ("Islamic Party" formed by Gulbuddin Hekmatyar)

HIK	Hezb-e Islami Khalis ("Islamic Party" formed by Mohammad Yunus Khalis)
ICRC	International Committee of the Red Cross
IDLG	Independent Directorate for Local Governance
IED	Improvised Explosive Devices
IO	International Organization
IRoA	Islamic Republic of Afghanistan
ISAF	International Security Assistance Force
ISI	Inter-Service Intelligence (Pakistan)
Karez	A small underground irrigation system popular in Afghanistan
LGCD	Local Governance and Community Development Program
Meshrano Jirga	Elders' Assembly, upper house of Afghan National Assembly
MRRD	Ministry of Rural Rehabilitation and Development
Mustafiat	Department of Finance
NDS	National Directorate for Security
NGO	Non-Governmental Organization
NSP	National Solidarity Program
NWFP	North West Frontier Province
Pashtunwali	The Pashtuns' pre-Islamic code of conduct
PC	Provincial Council
PDC	Provincial Development Council
PDP	Provincial Development Plan
PRT	Provincial Reconstruction Team
UN	United Nations
UNAMA	United Nations Assistance Mission in Afghanistan
UNOPS	United Nations Office for Project Services
USACE	US Army Corp of Engineers
USAID	US Agency for International Development
USDA	US Department of Agriculture
Wali	Governor
Wolesi Jirga	People's Assembly, lower house of Afghan National Assembly
Woluswal	District Administrator

Guide to the Handbook

This handbook is a concise field guide to Paktya for internationals deploying to the province. Field personnel have used these guides in Afghanistan since June 2008 to accelerate their orientation process and to serve as a refresher on different aspects of the province during their tour.

Reading this book will provide a basic understanding of the people, places, history, culture, politics, economy, needs, and ideas of Paktya. Building upon this understanding can help you:

- Build rapport and a regular dialogue with local leaders,

- Plan and implement pragmatic strategies (security, political, economic) to address sources of instability,

- Influence communities to support the political process, not the insurgents, and

- Build the capacity and legitimacy of a self-sufficient Afghan government and economy.

As you read the handbook and continue your inquiry in the province, seek to understand the influential leaders and groups in your local area and what beliefs and relationships drive their behavior. Think about the sources of violence in the area and whether groups are pursuing interests in a way that promotes conflict or stability. Finally, consider how various types of activities – key leader engagement, development assistance, security operations, security assistance, or public diplomacy – can effectively influence communities to work within the political process and oppose insurgency.

SOURCES AND METHODS

These handbooks are not intended as original academic research but as concise, readable summaries for practitioners in the field. The editorial team relies on its collective field experience and knowledge of the province as well as key sources such as the official Islamic Republic of Afghanistan (IRoA), United Nations, and United States Government (USG) publications, and those sources listed in the appendix.

The editors made every effort to ensure accuracy. It should be noted, however, that there is often considerable disagreement regarding what is "ground truth" in Paktya and things are constantly changing. As such, consider this book part of your orientation, and not an all-inclusive source for everything you need to know.

Information in this handbook is unclassified. The views and opinions expressed in this handbook are those of IDS International and in no way reflect the views of the United States Government or the United States Army.

THE ELECTRONIC UPDATE

Look for electronic updates to this book at *www.idsinternational.net/ afpakbooks*. Updates will cover new developments, issues, and leaders that emerge after publication. They will also provide corrections and expanded content in key areas based on input from readers.

We hope the handbook will continue to be a valuable tool in thinking about the challenges in Paktya. If you have questions, comments, or feedback for future updates or editions please email *afpakbooks@idsinternational.net*.

ABOUT IDS INTERNATIONAL

Publisher of Afghanistan and Pakistan Provincial Handbooks Series

This book is part of a series of handbooks on Afghanistan and Pakistan provinces and regions. Afghanistan province titles include Nuristan, Kunar, Nangarhar, Laghman, Khost, Paktika, Ghazni, Helmand, and Kandahar. Pakistan province titles include North West Frontier Province (NWFP) and the Federally Administered Tribal Areas (FATA).

In addition to publishing these handbooks, IDS International provides training and analysis to government and private organizations in the areas of politics, economics, culture, stability operations, reconstruction, counterinsurgency, and interagency relations. In particular, IDS is a leading trainer of the US military in working with Provincial Reconstruction Teams (PRTs) in Iraq and Afghanistan. IDS offers its clients expertise and experience in the difficult work of interagency collaboration in complex operations. The writers and editors on this project offer a lifetime of experience working in these provinces and share a dedication to bringing peace and prosperity to the people of Afghanistan.

Authors: Tom Praster
Editors: Amy Frumin and Scott Stanford
Assistant Editors: Tom Viehe, Chris Hall, and Emily Rose

IDS INTERNATIONAL GOVERNMENT SERVICES

1916 Wilson Boulevard

Suite 302

Arlington, VA 22201

703-875-2212

www.idsinternational.net

afpakbooks@idsinternational.net

PUBLISHED: MAY 2010

This and other AfPak handbooks may be purchased in either hard copy or digital format. Samples are available upon request. IDS International is also a leading provider of training and support on the cultural, political, economic, interagency and information aspects of conflict. For inquires, please email *afpakbooks@idsinternational.net* or call 703-875-2212.

Built by the British in the 19th century, 'Castle Greyskull' is currently occupied by the Afghan National Army. According to local myth, the foundations of the fort were built during the time of Alexander the Great.

PHOTO BY TOM PRASTER

Chapter 1
Overview and Orientation

Paktya is the heartland of the Pashtuns and spans the gamut of Pashtun lifestyles. Indeed, the name Paktya derives from the word "Pakthun," an alternative pronunciation of Pashtun. In the far southwest, farmers turn desert into farmland through the use of the famous, ancient Afghan karez, canals running for miles underground throughout the province. As one moves northeast up through the central valley, the land gets steeper on all sides. Here, the only agriculture is near the rivers, with terraced farms notched into the mountainsides. In the higher elevations, men illegally cut timber for export and drive firewood and pinecones in precariously-loaded jingle trucks down the streambeds to market. The high elevations also provide refuge to smugglers, bandits, and insurgents, which are perhaps the oldest professions in these mountains. Operation Anaconda, the first large-scale American fight in Afghanistan, took place in the highlands of southeast Paktya.

Paktya is 90 percent Pashtun, with some of the most famous of the Pashtun tribes – Ahmadzai, Zazi, Mangal, Zadran, Chamkani, Kharoti, Andar, and Tuta Khel – occupying distinct areas in the province. A host of smaller tribes – Sahak, Saleh Khel, Momozee, Dawlatzi, Ureakhail, Menzi, Mohsinkhel, Nekbikhel, Kotikhel, Karmashi, Hasankai, Salu Khel, Malak Khel, Shakar Khel, Ahengaran, Ziori, Sadaat, Kochi

Khail, Raees Khel, Salat Beg, Khawaja Hasan, and Shekhan, as well as Kuchis (not formally considered a tribe) – are concentrated in northern Zormat and into southern Gardez districts.

Paktya is a conservative province; it is rare to see a woman, even in the capital city Gardez, without a burkha, and the call to prayer is observed with few exceptions. Many of the Taliban's core leaders and supporters are from the villages of Paktya and initially the province welcomed the Taliban. However, the Taliban fell out of favor with the population due to their oppressive policies and tactics. When the Taliban fell, local warlords feuded over the province, and the unrest of that period affects the province to this day.

Trucks, phones, farming equipment, gas operated generators, radios, and guns have brought some elements of modernity to parts of the province, but in many ways life goes on as it has for centuries. Common scenes, such as a caravan of camels and sheep, or a robed man leading a woman on a donkey, allow one to imagine what it was like to be here almost three thousand years ago when Alexander the Great's men came to these same lands. The heartland of the Pashtuns is still a place where friends will find strong allies and enemies are implacable foes.

ORIENTATION

Paktya is roughly rectangular, with the long sides running south-west to northeast. It borders Nangarhar to the north, Logar to the northwest, Ghazni to the west, Paktika to the southwest, and Khost to the southeast. It shares a 100 kilometer international boundary with Kurram Agency in Pakistan's Federally Administered Tribal Areas (FATA) to the northeast. Paktya's central valley begins near its northeast edge and gradually broadens to the full width of the province in the southwest. The provincial capital, Gardez, sits in the middle of the valley. From the capital, roads run northwest to Kabul, east to Khost, and south to Zormat. Roads leading to the northeastern districts and the Pakistan border are being paved with some difficulty due to the constant threat of improvised explosive devices (IEDs).

The province is about the same size as Delaware, covering 6,432 square kilometers. For the 2003 elections, the population was estimated at 470,000, and Paktya received only five delegates in the lower house of parliament. However, nearly 400,000 people voted, indicating that the United Nations (UN) estimate of 1.1 million people was likely more accurate.

The climate is one of extremes, with hot, dry summers, and cold winters. Heavy winter snows used to be a feature of the area but are now rare. With meager spring melts for most of the last 20 years, rivers have been low, wells have gone dry, and irrigation has become more difficult. Farm yields have dropped and many farmers have sold off livestock or abandoned farming altogether to move to the towns and cities. Aside from minor marble and chromite deposits, Paktya's main resources are people, land, water, and timber.

Districts

There are 11 official and three unofficial districts in Paktya. The unofficial districts have been set up by local and provincial officials and the US military works with their provincially-appointed representatives. These three unofficial districts, however, have not been codified by the central government. Northern Sayed Karam, Ahmad Abad, Mirzaka (unofficial), Ahmad Khel (unofficial), and Zazi are located in the mountainous highlands of northeastern Paktya. Lija Mangal, Chamkani, Dand Wa Patan, Jani Khel, Waza Zadran, Shwak, and Gerda Serai (unofficial) constitute the central and southern mountainous

Map 1. Population Map of Paktya

Legend:
- Roads
- District Border
- River
- ⊙ Provincial Center
- • City

LESS ◄——————► MORE

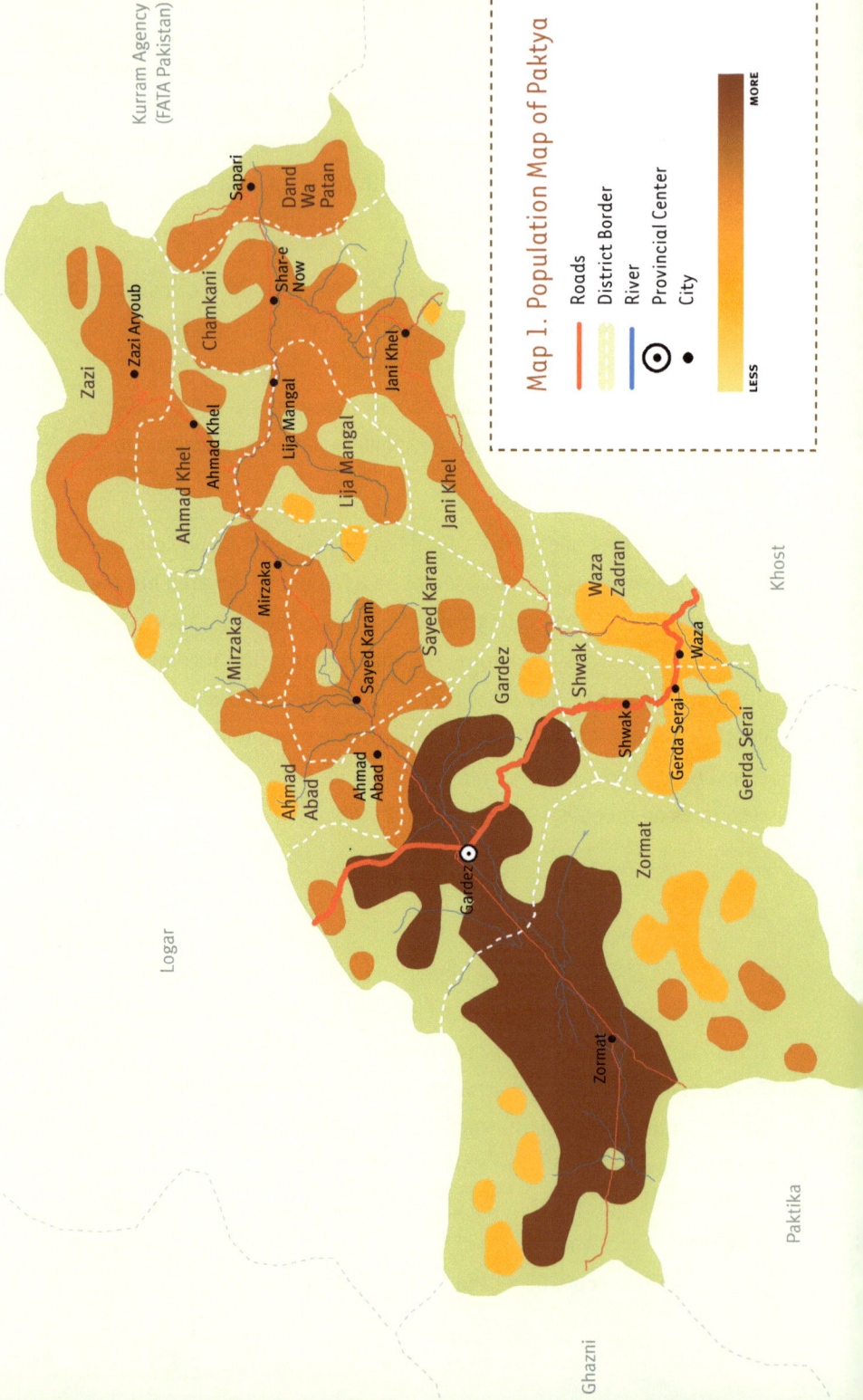

Kurram Agency
(FATA Pakistan)

Sapari

Dand Wa Patan

Zazi Aryoub

Chamkani

Zazi

Share Now

Jani Khel

Ahmad Khel

Ahmad Khel

Lija Mangal

Lija Mangal

Jani Khel

Mirzaka

Mirzaka

Sayed Karam

Waza Zadran

Sayed Karam

Gardez

Shwak

Waza

Mirzaka

Sayed Karam

Shwak

Waza

Khost

Gerda Serai

Ahmad Abad

Ahmad Abad

Gardez

Gerda Serai

Logar

Zormat

Zormat

Paktika

Ghazni

areas. The remaining three, together with parts of Zormat and six other districts in Khost and Paktika, form the infamous "Zadran Arc," a region renowned for resisting foreign incursions. Farming in these districts uses terraced plots located along mountain streams. Villagers also collect firewood and pinecones (for the pine nuts) which jingle trucks transport down the perilous mountain roads to the market. The valley starting in Chamkani and spilling through Dand Wa Patan into Pakistan is different – its lower elevation allows for more open-field farming.

From south to north, Zormat, Gardez, and southern Sayed Karam form the central valley of Paktya. There is some desert in the south, but most is fertile farmland fed from the Jilga River or deep wells. Wheat, corn, and alfalfa are the predominant crops. Most of the valley is free of any organized insurgency, but there are regular, if ineffective, attacks on Gardez. Gardez and Sayed Karam also host important insurgent facilitators. Zormat is the birthplace of many Taliban leaders, and is insurgent-controlled. The Shah-i-Kot Valley, scene of Operation Anaconda in 2002, is in the mountains of southern Zormat. Several reports in the international media of serious mistreatment and even death of Zormatis detained by US forces have made it difficult to gain support for coalition forces and the central government.

Increasingly, there are insurgency problems in Zazi (sometimes spelled Jaji) that spill over into Ahmad Khel. The districts near Pakistan in the northeast and south are even more problematic, offering routes and sanctuaries for anti-Afghan forces (AAF) transiting to Kabul or their hideouts in Logar.

Key Towns

Gardez was once the capital of Loya Paktya, or greater Paktya, a province comprised of modern day Paktya, Paktika, and Khost. After Paktika and Khost were made into separate provinces (in the 1970s and 1990s respectively), Gardez declined in importance. The first American forces to enter the city dubbed the brooding fort that dominates the city "Castle Greyskull." Currently occupied by the Afghan National Army (ANA), the main walls of the fort were built by the British in the 19th century, while legend (almost certainly apocryphal) dates its foundations to Alexander the Great. Across the road, the police headquarters sits on a prominent hill. Otherwise, the city is unremarkable. Several streets are now paved, but many still turn to mud in the winter and spring.

Since 2003, however, Gardez has benefited from its location on a main road leading to Kabul and from the relative stability in the surrounding valley. It now has a boomtown atmosphere following the establishment of a coalition forward operating base (FOB), the Provincial Reconstruction Team (PRT), an Afghan National Army (ANA) barracks, a police Regional Training Center, and the opening of a new university downtown. In January 2008, then-governor Rahmat noted, "There were 400 shops in Gardez four years ago, but now there are 1,400 shops. Sixty high-rise buildings have been built in the town. Twenty-one kilometers of road have been repaired in different districts of Gardez town, and residential houses are being built for 1,000 families." Ongoing efforts to improve the Gardez -Ghazni road and the Khost-Gardez road will also improve the city's economy.

Zormat, the center for the district of the same name, is a small market town. Starting in the Communist era, it gained a reputation as a center for anti-government activity, which continues today. This reputation has driven away many of the businessmen who used to trade extensively with India, and today Zormat is relatively poor.

Table 1: District Populations

DISTRICT	DISTRICT CENTER	POPULATION	MAJOR TRIBES
Ahmad Abad	Ahmad Abad	75,000	Ahmadzai
Ahmad Khel (unofficial)	Ahmad Khel	80,000	Zazi
Chamkani	Shar-e Now	110,000	Chamkani
Dand Wa Patan	Sapari	65,000	Mangal, Zazi
Gerda Serai (unofficial)	Gerda Serai	63,000	Zadran
Gardez	Gardez	118,000	Ahmadzai, Tajik, mixed
Jani Khel	Jani Khel	70,000	Mangal
Lija Mangal	Lija Mangal	65,000	Mangal
Mirzaka (unofficial)	Mirzaka	Unknown	Mangal, Ahmadzai
Sayed Karam	Sayed Karam	80,000	Tuta Khel
Shwak	Shwak	45,000	Zadran
Waza Zadran	Waza	70,000	Zadran
Zazi	Zazi Aryoub	95,000	Zazi
Zormat	Zormat	175,000	Andar, Zadran, Kharoti, mixed
TOTAL		1,111,000	

Note: These figures are from the Department of Disaster Preparedness. They are only estimates, and should be used with care, but are the closest estimates that seem to agree with voter registration data.

Shar-e Now, the district center for Chamkani, is important because of its proximity to the mouth of the valley that opens into Pakistan. Due to its isolation from Gardez, special efforts are required to maintain government control in the area. There is another American FOB in Chamkani, and ISAF has provided transportation to the ministerial representatives at the provincial level (referred to as line directors) into the area as a means to extend the reach of the government into this remote area and keep it allied with the government.

RELEVANT HISTORICAL ISSUES

From Ancient to Modern Times

Archaeological sites in Paktya have uncovered evidence of Indo-Greek, Sassanid, Hephalite, Turki-Shahi, and Hindu cultures. The earliest mention of Gardez is in the medieval *Tarikh-e Sistan*, which refers to the Islamic conquest of the city. The area that is now Paktya was part of the Aflahid Dynasty and a center of Kharijite belief for more than a century. The Kharijites were a Muslim sect separate from Sunni and Shia that believed in the individual's right to interpret Islam. Sometimes called Shurats, their only remaining enclave is in Iraq. In 870, the Saffid ruler Yaqub bin Layt took control of the region which was later conquered by the Ghaznawi Dynasty in the 10th century. In 1162, Gardez fell to the Sultans of Ghor, and by the 16th century it was part of the Mughal Empire.

During the 19th century wars with Britain, control of eastern Afghanistan changed hands several times. When the issue was finally settled in 1893, the Pashtun homelands were divided by the Durand Line. This disputed border was drawn by Britain and signed by the Afghan king under duress. Pashtuns claim the border was to expire after 100 years, but there is nothing in the treaty or the historical record on that point. As with many of the Pashtun tribes, several Paktya-based tribes straddle the international border, and do not accept it unless it serves their purpose.

In 1929, the Mangal tribe of Loya Paktya helped Mohammad Nadir Shah overthrow the Tajik king of Afghanistan, Habibullah Kalakani, thus returning the monarchy to Pashtun hands. In recognition of their contribution, the king granted the people of Loya Paktya an exemption from state taxes and military conscription, and promised them minimal state intervention and the right to bear arms. Despite the king's assassination four years later, this agreement was upheld until the central government began building roads and schools in the province in the 1950s. This sudden involvement by the national government sparked a tribal revolt led by the Mangal tribe. The government quickly withdrew and accepted the status quo.

Communist Era (1979-1992)

Paktya was the birthplace of noted leftists, including Najibullah Ahmadzai (the last Communist president of Afghanistan, who was hanged by the Taliban in 1996) and Mohammad Aslam Watanjar (the military commander in Kabul during the communist coup in 1979). Ironically, it is also the home to several prominent mujahedin, some of whom are now part of the insurgency, including Mullah Maulavi Nasrullah Mansoor, a leading member of the Taliban who is an important figure throughout the region (originally from Khost), and Jalaludin Haqqani, an early member of Hezb-e Islami Khalis and now the leader of his own militia network. There are also stories of a young Osama bin Laden fighting in the area of Ayroub during this timeframe.

Early mujahedin attacks were cautious night attacks on schools and district centers. They soon evolved into IED and ambush attacks on Soviet forces. Eventually, Maulavi Mansoor gained a foothold in south-west Zormat district, and fought several battles there. In the north, Gulbudin Hekmatyar and Abddurab Rasoul Sayaf held the mountain redoubt of Speena Shaga in Chamkani against strong government attacks. Haqqani was the first mujahid to capture a city (Khost) from the Soviets, and he is trying to use the same tactics in the Khost-Gardez pass today. He also fought several battles around Gardez from 1990-1992.

Mujahedin and the Taliban (1992-2001)

When the communist government fell, a shura was established in Paktya which included, among others, Haqqani (also the central government Minister of Justice), Maulavi Mansoor, and two local commanders: Ziauddin Dildar and Abdulla. This arrangement caused chaos as various militias roamed the province; it collapsed when the Taliban came to power in 1994. The order the Taliban brought was initially welcomed in the province. Soon, however, many people began to resent the Taliban's dogmatic, repressive interpretation of Islam. When the anti-Taliban forces attacked in 2001, the Taliban found little support among the majority of the population.

Contemporary Events (2001-present)

The Taliban did not flee Paktya completely in 2001. Many of them gathered in the Shah-i-Kot Valley in southern Zormat. In early March 2002 Operation Anaconda saw 1,700 US troops and 1,000 Afghan militia battle more than 1,000 al-Qaeda and Taliban fighters to obtain control of the valley. Maulavi Saifur Rehman Mansoor, the son of Mullah Maulavi Nasrullah Mansoor, led the Taliban reinforcements. While the US held the ground at the end of the day and suffered far fewer losses than the Taliban, the main Taliban force was able to successfully retreat into Pakistan or melt back into the population.

When the Taliban left Gardez in 2001, civil war broke out between Pacha Khan Zadran (PKZ), a tribal elder, and the Tajik minority centered in Gardez, represented by Ziauddin and Abdulla. By 2003, the government was backing the Tajiks; Ziauddin was a brigade commander in the Afghan Provisional Army, and Abdulla was chief of police in Paktya. Pacha Khan hid with his men in the mountains between Gardez and Khost when the provincial governorship he was promised did not materialize. Sporadic violence broke out, sometimes involving US troops, including a skirmish in which one of PKZ's sons was killed. PKZ fled to Pakistan, where in 2004 he was arrested by the police and extradited to Kabul. There he made his peace with President Karzai, and was later elected to parliament for Paktya. His son, Abdul Wali, is the district sub-governor of Waza Zadran. In the meantime, Ziauddin and Abdulla were arrested for corruption and conspiring against the government. Ziauddin spent approximately a year in prison in Bagram; Abdulla spent three years in Guantanamo Bay. Neither has returned to Paktya.

Despite this progress, security remains a problem in the province. During the 2004 elections, rockets were fired at a helicopter bringing President Karzai to address a rally in Gardez. In September 2006, Governor Taniwal was killed just outside his Gardez office by a suicide bomber. In July 2009, six suicide bombers attacked government buildings in Gardez. At the headquarters of the National Directorate of Security (NDS), a bomber detonated his explosives and killed three intelligence officers. Two other attackers were killed before they could detonate their explosives. At the governor's office, two bombers were shot to death by guards before they could set off their explosives and the last attacker headed for the police station was also killed. Two police officers were killed in the attacks.

The Haqqani Network (and remnants of the Mansoor organization) are openly operating throughout southern Paktya, predominately in the K-G Pass districts and the Zormat district. There have been numerous attacks against coalition forces, including an IED ambush in June 2008 that killed two US soldiers from the PRT. Zormati officials claim they could curb the violence if coalition forces would not be so heavy-handed. The international press, Human Rights Watch, and other NGOs have documented several cases where US forces arrested Zormatis who either died in custody or were later released for lack of evidence after long incarcerations. Some remain in the detention system but local officials are unable to trace them or learn the charges against them.

The Haqqani Network, now controlled primarily by his son Sirajuddin, and Hezb-e-Islami Gulbudin (HIG) continue to operate throughout Paktya, although the border regions (Haqqani in the central and HIG in the north) see the most activity. In July 2008, reportedly one of Haqqani's sons and two sisters were killed by a US airstrike in eastern Gardez province. Maulavi Saifur Rehman Mansoor's influence as a Taliban commander has waned, despite the fact that his father was a respected mullah and mujahedin.

How These Issues Affect Paktya Today

Just like the mujahedin's fight against the Soviets, the Taliban opposition to coalition forces started slowly, using night letters and unsophisticated, timer-based rocket attacks that were safe for the attacker because he could leave the area hours in advance. Over time, the Taliban have grown bolder, with an ability to strike anywhere in the province with IEDs, and to conduct frontal attacks against isolated border outposts and district centers. The Soviet response to these tactics, massive retaliations with the complete destruction of many villages, was unsuccessful and thus potentially instructive in terms of what not to do.

Continued attacks against government officials justify the concerns of line directors and sub-governors, who are often afraid to stray far from their office compounds. Unrest in Zormat continues, with tensions heightened by the many Zormatis who, as mentioned above, have been arrested in recent years by coalition forces.

Ethnically, Paktya is dominated by Pashtuns, who follow an honor code known as 'pashtunwali.' The Zadrans are the largest Pashtun tribe in the region, inhabiting an area known as the Zadran Arc, spanning Paktya, Paktika, and Khost.

PHOTO BY TOM PRASTER

Chapter 2
Ethnicity, Tribes,
Languages, and Religion

ETHNICITY

Pashtuns dominate Paktya, comprising an estimated 91 percent of the population. The Pashtuns are believed to be the largest tribal society in the world, with roughly 15 to 25 million people living in Afghanistan and Pakistan. Their code of honor, *pashtunwali*, serves as the cultural bedrock.

The remaining nine percent of the population is almost entirely Tajiks. Those living in the Tajik enclave around Gardez are the descendents of politicians and businessmen who migrated to the capital of Loya Paktya during periods of Tajik rule in Kabul. Both Pashtuns and Tajiks are Sunni Muslims. Ethnic tensions are generally not an issue in Paktya.

TRIBES

Tribes are the most important political units in eastern and southern Afghanistan. They have served as the basis for social organization in the region for centuries and remain powerful despite the fact that traditional tribal structures have been undermined by three decades

Table 2. Major Tribes in Paktya

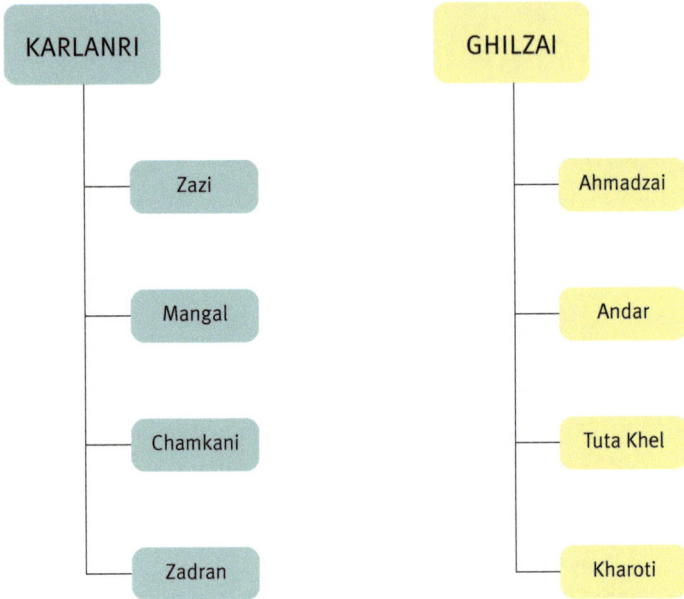

KARLANRI
- Zazi
- Mangal
- Chamkani
- Zadran

GHILZAI
- Ahmadzai
- Andar
- Tuta Khel
- Kharoti

of conflict. Tribes have gained importance in recent years as ordinary people sought ways to organize themselves outside of the weak Afghan government structures. Tribal identity is much more important than national identity – an Afghan Mangal will be more loyal to a Pakistani Mangal than he would be to an Afghan Tajik or Uzbek. The most revealing question you can ask any Paktyan is, "What tribe are you from?" The answer will give you a clue about loyalties that may cut across any other allegiance to political parties, business deals, or military affiliation.

The two basic institutions of the tribal system are the *jirga* and *shura*; a jirga is a tribal gathering to solve a problem or reach a decision, while a shura is a more permanent council of elders who can be responsible for security, justice, and local administration. Shuras can be organized geographically – village shuras are a well-established tradition, while district shuras are a formal part of the Afghan government – or they can be gathered along tribal lines. Each major tribe in Paktya has a shura to represent its interests, so you will frequently hear references to the Zazi shura or the Tuta Khel shura, for example.

Tribal leaders sometimes live in Gardez or Kabul, but depend on their support base in the villages. Determining who the leaders of a tribe are may, therefore, require some research beyond meeting with village elders. Also, it is important to understand the conditions in a politician's home district if you are to understand or predict his reaction to national and international events.

The Pashtun tribes in Paktya are broadly divided into Karlanri and Ghilzai "super tribes," as the chart on page 16 shows. The Karlanri are generally arrayed along both sides of the Durand Line. The fact that many of their tribes are divided keeps them in the center of Afghan/Pakistan relations. The Ghilzai initially formed the backbone of the early

Taliban movement, but that connection is no longer indicative of their political activities. Today, the Ghilzai sub-tribes vary in their affiliations.

Categorizing Pashtuns is a bit abstract to most Paktyans. Nobody would describe themselves as "Ghilzai" or "Karlanri"; instead, they would always use their specific tribal name, such as Tuta Khel. Even smaller divisions within the tribes can be politically important; some tribes divide along clan lines over whether they support or oppose the government. However, all still do consider themselves Afghan.

The map on page 20 shows which tribes are strongest in broad swaths of the province, but this information should be used with caution. Tribes are scattered across Paktya in a dense patchwork, dividing districts – and even villages – into distinct zones of control. Rival tribes can hold sway over neighboring clusters of houses in the same town.

It is therefore crucial to understand with whom one is dealing. A delegation that introduces itself as the "Khandar Khel shura" may represent only one clan from that village. Implementing a project on their behalf might alienate the rest of the district. Providing food assistance through one central point of contact in a district with several tribes could result in many areas being neglected.

Pashtunwali

Society in Paktya is very conservative, strictly religious, and structured around "pashtunwali." Pashtunwali means "the way of the Pashtuns," and is a pre-Islamic code of conduct followed by the Pashtun tribes. All Pashtuns have some knowledge of the code and will try to follow it. Some tribes are stricter about the code than others. The four main parts of Pashtunwali are as follows:

Nang (Honor): All parts of Pashtunwali lead to Honor. All Pashtuns are required to uphold the honor of their family and their tribe by following the other parts of the code. An insult to someone's tribe or family can lead to Badal *(see below)*. The biggest disputes are over women, land, and money; and a Pashtun man must protect all three with his life and honor.

Melmastia (Hospitality): Pashtuns are known for their hospitality and will go to great lengths to treat their guest with honor and respect. Most villages and large families will have a dedicated guesthouse. Even if a family has limited resources, a stranger will still be welcomed, fed, and given a place to sleep. This applies to non-Pashtuns as well.

Nanawatay (Sanctuary): If one Pashtun has insulted or committed a crime against another, they are allowed to admit their guilt and ask for forgiveness. They will take gifts to the offended party and ask that the past be forgotten. The insulted party is then obligated to accept their offer. Often the women of a family or tribe will arrange for this to happen because women are seen as natural peacemakers. Nanawatay can also be used to beg for mercy and protection.

Badal (Revenge): Pashtuns are quick to take revenge for an insult or seek justice for a past crime. It does not matter if the insult is decades old. The only way to restore honor to one's family/clan/tribe is to exact revenge on the other's family/clan/tribe.

Prominent Tribes of Paktya

There is some dispute regarding the extent to which tribal affiliations can be used as an indicator of an individual's disposition towards the Afghan government and coalition forces. Loyalties can and do shift often in Afghanistan. That said, the descriptions below highlight those tribal leaders who are closely aligned with the Afghan Government.

Map 2. Tribal Map of Paktya

Legend:

—	Roads
---	District Border
~	River
⊙	Provincial Center
•	City

Tribes:
- Kharoti
- Mangal
- Mixed Tribes
- Tajik
- Tuta Khel
- Zadran
- Zazi
- Andar
- Ahmadzai
- Chamkani

Labels on map:

Kurram Agency (FATA Pakistan)

Sapari
Dand Wa Patan
Zazi
Zazi Aryoub
Chamkani
Shar-e Now
Ahmad Khel
Ahmad Khel
Lija Mangal
Lija Mangal
Jani Khel
Jani Khel
Mirzaka
Mirzaka
Sayed Karam
Sayed Karam
Ahmad Abad
Ahmad Abad
Gardez
Shwak
Waza Zadran
Waza
Shwak
Gerda Serai
Gerda Serai
Gardez
Zormat
Zormat
Khost
Logar
Ghazni
Paktika

Concentrated in Ahmad Abad, Mirzaka, northern Gardez district, and the two districts to the north, a large portion of the **Ahmadzai** were traditionally nomadic Kuchi. This ancestry accounts for their wide distribution over southeastern Afghanistan and their reputation as fierce warriors. As one of the largest tribes in Paktya, the Ahmadzai's support for the GIRoA is a significant factor in the stability of central Paktya.

Residents of arid Zormat, the **Andar** have become famous for the extent and complexity of their *karezes*, the Afghan system of underground irrigation. Although conservative Sunnis, the Andar aligned themselves for a time with the Shia Harakat-i Islami during the anti-Soviet campaign.

The **Zazi** (or Jaji) are found primarily in the district of the same name. Hill men, they are famous for their unique dances. Many Zazi are supporters of Abdul Sayyaf, the conservative warlord who was aligned with the Northern Alliance. Daoud Zazi, a well-known Zazi mujahed, now represents the province in the Wolesi Jirga (lower house of Parliament).

The **Kharoti** clan is known as good businessmen. The majority of Kharoti live in Paktika, but there is an enclave in southern Zormat. Interestingly, two prominent insurgent leaders, Gulbuddin Hekmatyar and Harakat are Kharoti, but in general the Kharoti are known as strong supporters of the government.

The **Mangal** are fiercely independent, and were cited in many foreigners' journals for their exploits against the British. They enhanced that reputation fighting the Soviets and the Taliban, and continue to be a strong anti-Taliban force. The tribe stretches from Lija Mangal, across Jani Khel, and into Dand Wa Patan. They are in a running feud with the Tuta Khel *(see below)*. Paktya Deputy Governor Mangal comes from this tribe.

The Kuchi are a migratory ethnic group who travel throughout Afghanistan and have special representation within the national government. Some tribes, like the Ahmadzai, trace their lineage to the Kuchi, which explains their wide distribution over large swaths of land.

PHOTO BY TOM PRASTER

Another northern tribe known for its smuggling prowess, the **Chamkani** farms the fertile valley in the Chamkani district just across the Pakistan border. Generally considered pro-government, the tribe is under considerable pressure, as it occupies a strategic area crucial to insurgent passage to and from Pakistan.

The **Tuta Khel** offer an interesting contrast – while generally supportive of the government, they also have a reputation for lawlessness. A favorite Tuta Khel tactic is to kidnap someone and take them to Pakistan until a ransom is paid. Their running rivalry with the Mangal is motivated by the Tuta Khel's checkpoints on local roads. Both sides participate in the feud, one side often raiding the other's village and burning houses. Sayed Karam and southern Mirzaka constitute the Tuta Khel homeland. Mullah Haji Jailani, one of the most prominent Haqqani sub-commanders to take advantage of the government's amnesty program for its former opponents, Program Tahkim-e-Solh (PTS), is a Tuta Khel.

The **Zadran** tribe is the largest Pashtun tribe in southeastern Afghanistan. Present in many districts in Paktya, it is concentrated in Waza Zadran, Shawak, Gerda Serai, and Zormat districts. Pacha Khan Zadran is one of the most famous of the Zadran tribe. Insurgent leader Jalaludin Haqqani is another influential member of the Zadran tribe. Zadran tribesmen constitute a large percentage of the insurgent forces in Paktya.

LANGUAGES

All Paktyans speak Pashto. Tajiks and government leaders from outside the province will sometimes speak Dari, Afghanistan's other official language, as their first language, but all will understand Pashto. Words from Urdu and Arabic have become part of Pashto, but neither language is commonly spoken in the province.

ROLE OF RELIGION

The vast majority of Paktyans are deeply devoted to Sunni Islam. Residents of Paktya strictly observe the rituals and requirements of their faith. No outsider should ever speak poorly about Islam or accuse an Afghan of being un-Islamic. It is good to compliment someone for being a good Muslim, but the topic of religion should be approached lightly, if at all. Since the Koran is seen by Muslims as an infallible document, delivered to The Prophet directly by God, any debate on particulars of Islamic belief and practice should not be entered.

Since Afghanistan is an Islamic Republic, there is no separation between religion and government. A law must be in line with Islamic principles for it to be accepted. Religious elites have not historically ruled the province, but have played an important role in legitimizing leaders. Religious figures have intervened during times of crisis, however, and this pattern repeated itself in 1994 when the Taliban seized control and imposed a simple village version of Islamic order on the chaotic civil war. The mullahs lost power when the Taliban were toppled in 2001, and the current government's attempts to bring religious leaders back into the power structure have not been entirely successful. Maulvi Abdul Ghafoor is the Director of Religious Affairs, and is the government's official representative for the mullah community in the province. A total of 54 imams of local mosques are registered with the department, 22 of whom are based outside Gardez City. The official Ulema Shura, led by Maulvi Khaliqdad, is a group of religious scholars that supports the government. It has been willing to meet with coalition forces to suggest how they might better approach religious and security issues in the province. Due to their influence, reaching out to the mullahs directly or through their hierarchy is recommended.

Madrassas (religious schools) are a popular method of education because they generally provide students (all males) with room and board. There are 16 officially-registered madrassas in the province teaching a curriculum approved by the government. One reason for their formation was to provide an alternative to the refugee-camp madrassas in Pakistan, many of which have a radical curriculum and are a recruiting source for the insurgency. However, an indeterminate number of unofficial village madrassas teaching more extreme views have been founded in Paktya, and some villagers still send their sons for religious education in Pakistan, where some are indoctrinated to fight against infidels.

Officially, the national government is meant to have extensive control in the provinces. In practice, Kabul has never exerted substantial authority in Paktya, though its control of security and aid funding requires people to work with the government for these benefits.

PHOTO BY TOM PRASTER

Chapter 3
Government and Leadership

Paktya has had six governors since 2002. This lack of continuity has hindered the efforts of the central government to extend its reach into the province. In turn, the lack of established governance, especially in terms of a functioning police and justice system, and the slow pace of reconstruction and development, are often cited as the reasons for locals' dissatisfaction with the Karzai administration. Until a more effective provincial government is in place, tribal leadership will provide a parallel structure for governance, administering justice and providing security.

HOW THE GOVERNMENT OFFICIALLY WORKS

Central Control

Authority and power in Afghanistan are concentrated in the national government as a means to counter the power of warlords in the provinces. As such, the provincial government is limited to an advisory role for the central government, while decisions on everything from policy to funding priorities are made in Kabul.

Parliament

The Afghan National Assembly is comprised of two houses. The upper house is the *Meshrano Jirga* (Elders' Assembly), with 102 delegates – one-third elected by Provincial Councils, one-third by District Councils and one-third appointed by the president. The lower house is the *Wolesi Jirga* (People's Assembly) with 239 directly-elected delegates. Additional seats are set aside for women, handicapped and the nomadic Kuchi whom the president appoints. The National Assembly passes laws and the government's budget and approves government ministers before they take up their positions.

Provincial Government

A governor (*wali*) heads the provincial government and reports to the Independent Directorate for Local Governance (IDLG) located in the Executive Office of the President. Governors are currently appointed by the IDLG, not elected, which can impact their relationship with the people of the province. The governor is assisted by a deputy and several staff who oversee provincial government management. He is given a small budget to run his office but has no budget for projects. Generally, the governor's role is undefined in the Constitution, meaning their power depends on their personal influence with the central government and local population, their relationship with the PRT and international actors in the province, and any private sources of money and power.

The 25 ministries in Kabul execute their policies and programs through departments located at the provincial level. Ministers, with the approval of the president, appoint provincial directors who manage the department. The director reports to and receives funds from the ministry in Kabul. Although the provincial governor must approve all expenditures before they are processed by the Department of Finance (*Mustafiat*), he is not in the chain of command for the directors nor does he have budgetary authority over any of these departments.

The Provincial Council (PC) is the only democratically-elected body at the provincial level but it only plays an advisory role on provincial issues. The PC reports directly to the president but has no budget. However, a 2007 constitutional amendment gave the Provincial Council authority to approve the Provincial Development Plan (PDP), allowing them some capacity to be responsive to their constituents. Each province has completed a PDP laying out its goals for provincial development and is linked to the Afghan National Development Strategy (ANDS).

The Provincial Development Committee (PDC) is responsible for developing and overseeing the implementation of the PDP and is the forum for the coordination of development activity among local and international actors. The PDC is formally composed of provincial line directors and is chaired by the governor. The provincial Director of Economy is assigned to act as the Secretariat. The governor can invite PC members, elders, and members of the international community and the non-governmental community as non-voting members to ensure coordination among the various development actors active in the province. Participants often include the PRT, USAID, NGOs, the UN, and others active in the province. Ideally, Technical Working Groups (TWGs) are established by sector (in accordance with the sectors established in the ANDS) and can report their findings/recommendations to the PDC during its monthly meetings.

District and Local Governance

Government at the district level mirrors the provincial government with the *woluswal* (district administrator or sub-governor), police chief, National Directorate of Security officer, clerks, and a small police force. Ministry sub-departments also operate at the district level, but are not present in every district. In 2007, District Development Assemblies (DDA) were formed in order to plan, prioritize, and coordinate development activities at the district level and to feed local input into the provincial development planning process.

Recently, several provinces have begun establishing district shuras (sometimes translated as District Councils) under the Afghan Social Outreach Program (ASOP), which is run with the help of UNAMA. ASOP, overseen by the IDLG and funded by the US and UK, among others, hopes to empower local communities to engage with development issues, build social capital, channel the grievances of the people, and assume greater responsibility for local-level security. Under ASOP, council members would be paid 6,000 Af ($120) a month. The program has become controversial, as critics claim it is just an attempt by the central government to buy the loyalty of local leaders. Additionally, the manner in which district shura members are being chosen is unclear.

Below the district level, the only formal governance structures are Community Development Councils (CDCs) established under the National Solidarity Program (NSP). CDCs, however, do not have an established role in Afghan law.

The Municipality of Gardez is run by a mayor appointed by the IDLG in consultation with the governor. Municipalities are independent from the provincial government, are free to plan, fund, and implement projects, and can tax local businesses. There is often only one municipality in a province and it is usually also in the capital as the largest population center.

HOW IT ACTUALLY WORKS

No government from Kabul has ever been able to penetrate deeply into Paktya. The tribal system prevails as the dominant form of governance in Paktya due to the frequent changes in the governor's office, lack of adequate budget, inexperienced line directors, turmoil in the justice system, and unabated corruption. People continue to turn to tribal leaders to settle disputes and provide justice and, in some cases, security. Nevertheless, money for security programs and assistance projects will continue to be channeled through the formal government; if people want these benefits, they have to interact with the government.

Provincial Government

Governor Hamdard was appointed in December of 2008 to replace Rahmatullah Rahmat, who had served for only a year and proved ineffective. In Paktya, Hamdard developed a good relationship with coalition forces, the international community, and the NGO community, and appears to have a good relationship with Deputy Governor Mangal, the line directors, the Provincial Council, and security force leaders. However, he has not traveled extensively and has not yet established the relationships with the sub-governors and tribal leaders that are needed to govern effectively. Ironically, one reason that Hamdard has not had time to reach out more to tribes is that he is also Karzai's Adviser for Tribal Affairs, and spends considerable time in Kabul.

The Paktya Provincial Council does not have a strong leader, and the constant changeovers in governors have prevented it from forming a relationship with the governor which could help it to be a more relevant body. It has done little more than authorize the mandatory approval of the PDP. However, Governor Hamdard has been meeting regularly with the Council and it may play a greater role in the future.

Local Government

Independent village shuras sometimes administer security and operate their own informal court system without overt cooperation with either the insurgents or government. Such shuras have administered justice according to pashtunwali and, occasionally, Islamic law (sharia) for centuries, and provided for their security with *arbakai*, village militia called on in times of crisis. The government's attempts to supplant these traditions and impose a national solution in the form of federal law and national security forces are causing much of the tension in Paktya. When government institutions prove corrupt or fail to provide security, there is a strong desire to return to what has worked in the past, a desire which insurgents and radical mullahs play on to separate the people from the government.

A mayor, Engineer Agha Gul, heads the municipality of Gardez. The mayor is from Zormat, a traditional rival of Gardez. While his Zormat origins have created some resentment by the people, he is generally considered a good administrator and Gardez has grown and improved during his administration. However, people have protested his approved road renovations because they displaced some shopkeepers.

POLITICAL PARTIES

Most political parties in Afghanistan are little more than cliques formed around a charismatic personality or to promote a specific interpretation of Islam. Hence they tend not to play a significant role in the political process. Some of the more active in Paktya are listed in Table 3.

Table 3: Major Political Parties

PARTY NAME	NOTES
Hezb-e Islami Afghanistan (HIA)	Although sometimes still referred to as HIG (Hezb-e Islami Gulbuddin), this is the peaceful offshoot of that anti-government group. HIA recently opened an office in Gardez headed by Faizal Raib Jawhar, and has supporters throughout the province.
Hezb-e Islami Hekmatyar	Also similar to HIG, HIH has supporters in most of Paktya's districts.
Jamiat-e Islami	Popular among the Tajik, NDS chief is a member.
Mahaz-e Milli	A Jihadi party founded by Pir Gailani. Still enjoys some support in Paktya.
Jabha-e Nijat-e Milli	Headed by Sibghatullah al-Mojaddedi, now the director for reconciliation (PTS); the Gardez chief is Waquil Gulzar, a Zazi.
Ittehad-e Islami	Popular with Pashtuns when founded by Abdulrab Rasul Sayaf. It lost support after it aligned with the Northern Alliance.
Afghan Milat (Afghan Nation)	A Pashtun, anti-Tajik party that has grown in popularity as more people believe that Karzai has given too much authority to former Northern Alliance mujahedin. Led by Mohammed Rahim.
Harakat-e Islami Mohammadi	Located in Ahmad Abad, Sayed Karam districts
Harakat Islami Mansoor	Located in Zormat and Gardez center.
Hezb-e Islami Khalis	A jihadist party with supporters in Gerda Serai and Shwak
Ittehad-e Islami	A jihadist party with supporters in Zazi and Ahmad Khel

SECURITY FORCES

The official security actors in the province are the Afghan National Police (ANP) (within which there are several different police entities), the Afghan National Army (ANA), and the National Directorate for Security (NDS), which is akin to a combination of the American CIA and FBI. Ideally, commanders meet with ISAF on a regular basis to coordinate activities. Coordination Centers have been established by the US military and provide a location where coalition and Afghan forces can work together to monitor problems in real time. A Joint Provincial Coordination Center (JPCC) is located near the governor's compound, and Joint District Coordination Centers (JDCCs) are located in district capitals throughout the province.

Security Coordination

The Provincial Security Council, which includes coalition forces and all of the forces noted below, meets every two weeks to share intelligence and coordinate activities. Coalition participants report that the meetings are generally productive and Afghan representatives are very professional. While most provinces have their own Provincial Coordination Center near the governor's compound, Paktya coordination is done as part of the work of the Regional Coordination Center. The regional center covers Ghazni, Paktika, Logar, and Wardak and is housed at the ANA's headquarters.

Afghan National Army (ANA)

Paktya was one of the first provinces to receive an ANA deployment, and is now home to the 203rd "Thunder" Corps, headquartered in Gardez and commanded by General Abdul Khaliq. The presence of an ANA Corps, which combined with a special commando unit that works with Coalition Forces, brings the ANA troop level to approximately 2,600 troops. The ANA have thus played an important role in helping bring stability to the province.

Afghan National Police (ANP)

There are only 700 ANP in Paktya, although 1,300 are authorized. (To be precise, the term ANP includes the Afghan Uniformed Police (AUP), the Afghan National Civil Order Police (ANCOP), the Afghan Border Police (ABP), and the Afghan Highway police. However, most people use the term ANP to refer to just the AUP, and discuss the other groups separately. This book follows that convention unless otherwise noted.) The Paktya ANP was suffering from the same stigma of corruption and deficient training that follows the police throughout Afghanistan. After his appointment at the end of 2008, the professionalism of Provincial Chief of Police General Wardak impressed locals and international observers, and began to reverse this image. In most districts the ANP has regained some degree of respect. The high casualty rate the police are suffering as the frontline against the insurgents may have also played a role in changing Paktyans' image of their police force. Only in Zormat province, where the 70 police are significantly outnumbered by their enemies, was the ANP considered completely ineffective by international trainers. Unfortunately, growing concerns that Wardak has succumbed to corrupting influences is eroding progress throughout the province.

Table 4: Wolesi Jirga (Lower House) Members

NAME	TRIBE	POLITICAL PARTY	NOTES
Daud Zazai	Zazi Hasham Khel sub-tribe	Ittehad-e Islami	Sayyaf mujahidin commander, rumored to be close to ISI
Pacha Khan Zadran	Zadran	Jabha-e Nijat-e Milli	Extremely influential, especially in the south. His son is sub-governor of Waza Zadran
Fazal Rahman Chamkani***	Chamkani	N/A	HIG commander against Soviets. Former Director of Tribal Affairs
Gul Badshah Majidi	Zazi	Mahaz-e-Milli	Import/export business, no military background, living in Kabul
Sharifa Zormati	Pashtun, no further information	N/A	Journalist, living in Kabul

***Assassinated in April 2008, not yet replaced.*

National Directorate of Security (NDS)

The inner workings of Afghanistan's intelligence service, the NDS, are not publicly known. Paktyans often refer to the NDS as the KhAD, the name of the Ministry for State Security established under the Communist regime, and treat it with the same fearful deference. It is true that the NDS does rely on Russian-trained KhAD officers, most of whom are Tajik because the Pashtuns refused to cooperate with the Russians. Additionally, the director of the NDS in Kabul is Tajik. It is not hard to understand why many of the NDS officers in the provinces are Tajik, including its head and many of Paktya's NDS staff. While coalition forces that work with the NDS are generally impressed by the quality of its intelligence, there is a tendency by the Tajiks to sometimes mischaracterize Pashtun inter-tribal quarrels as insurgent activity in an attempt to separate the Pashtuns from the coalition.

LEADER PROFILES

Government Leaders

Juma Khan Hamdard, Governor: Appointed governor of Paktya in December 2008, Hamdard (51 years old) made his reputation as a commander in the north, fighting under Gulbuddin Hekmatyar. Allied with General Dostum in 1994 against the Taliban, he defected and contributed to Taliban victories over the Uzbek forces in 1997 and 1998. Later, Hamdard rejoined Dostum for the 2001 campaign that drove the Taliban out of the country.

Having proved an effective administrator as governor of Balkh, Hamdard was transferred to Jowzan, an Uzbek-dominated province in 2007. Dostum partisans led a series of protests against the appointment, and after a short period – during which he survived an assassination attempt, and 13 protestors were shot by police – he was assigned to Kunduz. However, protests there led to the cancellation of his appointment, and instead he was dispatched to Paktya. Born in Balkh, Hamdard is an ethnic Pashtun from the Dawlatzai tribe. He has a high school education, but his family status is unknown. Less than a year in office, Hamdard has demonstrated his capabilities, and his influence among the tribes is increasing.

Abdur Rahman Mangal, Deputy Governor: Mangal (46 years old) is from Lija Mangal in central Paktya. Prior to his appointment, he was the province's Director for Tribal Affairs and received high marks. He appears to be a good administrator and is effective in meetings when substituting for the governor.

Table 5: Meshrano Jirga (Upper House) Members

NAME	TRIBE	NOTES	CONTACT DETAILS
Sayed Hamed Gailani	Unknown	Son of Pir Gailani; serves as the First Deputy Speaker.	0700-275-538 0799-334-380 h_gailani@yahoo.com
Dr. Bahktar Aminzai	Unknown	Director of Martyr Service Charity and runs hospitals in Logar and Paktya.	0799-371-710 sen.aminzay@yahoo.com
Haji Mohammed Laiq	Unknown	From Chamkani district; not affiliated with a political party.	0799-097-425

General Aziz Wardak, Chief of Police: Appointed in the fall of 2008, he was a police chief in Wardak, and later held a position in Kabul. He initially impressed independent observers with his straightforward manner and his stated intention to bring more professionalism to the police force, and police morale improved. Unfortunately, there is increasing evidence he is corrupt.

General Ali Ahmed Mubaraz, Head of National Directorate of Security: General Mubaraz is a young Tajik who has cooperated closely with coalition forces in efforts to track Taliban in the province. However, he has a reputation as a self-serving careerist, and his motivation seems more anti-Pashtun than pro-government.

Pacha Khan Zadran, Member of Parliament: Pacha Khan was one of the last real warlords left standing in Paktya after the fall of the Taliban, and in the chaos that followed their departure he was appointed governor. When locals drove him out of office and Karzai's support for him waned, Pacha Khan began a two-year batttle against government and coalition forces, launching rockets into Gardez and closing the Khost-Gardez highway. During the rebellion one of his sons was killed by US forces. Pacha Khan was arrested in Pakisan in 2003, and deported to Kabul. There, he struck a deal with Karzai – he would turn in his militia's weapons in return for amnesty. Subsequently, he was elected to the Wolesi Jirga. A respected tribal elder in southeastern Paktya, Pacha Khan is still a powerful tribal leader, but has proven ineffective as a legislator. Despite his battles in the past with US forces, he has been willing to meet with US officials.

Sharifa Zormati Wardak, Member of Paliament: Sharifa Zormati is a respected female journalist who covered the Loya Jirga and women's issues prior to her election to the Wolesi Jirga in 2005.

Anti-Government Figures

Latif Rahman Mansoor: The nephew of deceased mujahedin commander Nasrullah Mansoor, he currently runs an anti-government network in Zormat associated with the Taliban.

Jalaludin Haqqani: From Gerda Sarai, Haqqani was governor of Paktya under the Taliban. He and his family are now based in Pakistan. Two of his sons have been killed, and another, Sirajuddin, has assumed control of the Haqqani Network.

Sirajuddin Haqqani: Sirajuddin is now the operational leader of the Haqqani Network. The network maintains close ties to Taliban leader Mullah Omar and al-Qaeda. Sirajuddin has admitted planning the January 14, 2008 attack against the Serena Hotel in Kabul that killed six people, including an American citizen. He also admitted to having planned the April 2008 assassination attempt on Afghan President Hamid Karzai. He regularly participates in cross-border attacks against Coalition Forces.

Shops selling basic house wares and implements can be found in any town in Paktya, serving the vast majority of Afghans who live in rural areas.

PHOTO BY TOM PRASTER

Chapter 4
The Economy

The economy of Paktya is not complicated. As with much of Afghanistan, most families depend upon farming, whether in a fertile valley or on a rugged mountain. War and drought have degraded Paktya's agricultural output and many are reduced to subsistence farming. Trade, mining, and crafts are minor contributors to the economy.

KEY SECTORS

Agriculture

Forty-five percent of the population is engaged in farming, most on relatively small one- to two-jerib plots (a jerib is 1/5 of a hectare). Paktya has been poppy free since 2004, and in 2008 Paktya received a million-dollar grant under the Ministry of Counter-Narcotics' Good Performers Initiative (GPI) for declining or nonexistent poppy production. The GPI is funded by, among others, USAID.

On the plains and wider river valleys of the south and extreme northeast, farmers grow wheat, corn, rice and other grains. Some of the farmland is irrigated by *karezes*, the underground tunnels connected by closely-spaced vertical shafts (known as *spargas*) which bring water to the surface from distant aquifers.

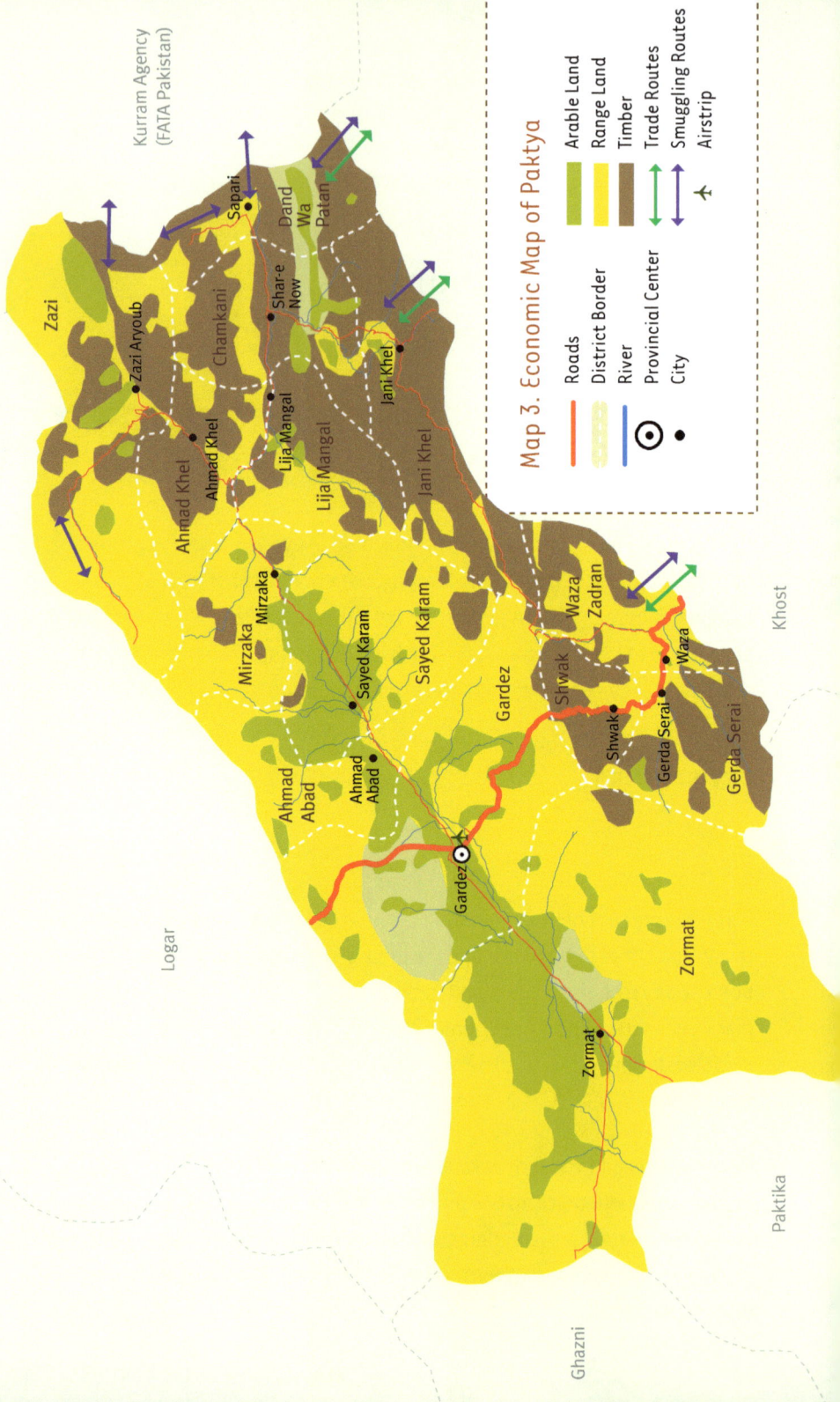

Map 3. Economic Map of Paktya

Roads
District Border
River
Provincial Center
City

Arable Land
Range Land
Timber
Trade Routes
Smuggling Routes
Airstrip

Kurram Agency (FATA Pakistan)

Zazi

Sapari

Dand Wa Patan

Chamkani

Shar-e Now

Zazi Aryoub

Ahmad Khel

Ahmad Khel

Lija Mangal

Lija Mangal

Jani Khel

Jani Khel

Mirzaka

Mirzaka

Sayed Karam

Sayed Karam

Waza Zadran

Waza

Shwak

Shwak

Gerda Serai

Gerda Serai

Gardez

Ahmad Abad

Ahmad Abad

Gardez

Khost

Logar

Zormat

Zormat

Ghazni

Paktika

In the mountains that surround the central valley, fruits, vegetables, and melons make up the majority of the crops. Grain is also grown on terraced plots. In the highlands of the southeast, the weather can prove too extreme or water too scarce for crops; instead, the major cash producer is timber, which is illegally exported to Pakistan. The pine forests are also a source of pinecones (pine nuts are a dietary staple in Paktya) and firewood to be sold as far away as Kabul. Unfortunately, the uncontrolled cutting (a national ban on timbering is not enforced) is rapidly destroying Paktya's forests. The mountains of the northwest are generally barren of forest coverage.

Thirty years of war have destroyed irrigation systems, orchards, mills, and storage facilities. Years of drought have also lowered the water table and increased the salinity of the soil. (Some experts believe lower precipitation may now be normal for Afghanistan.) As a result of these changes, farmers have been forced to reduce livestock herds and USAID has implemented efforts to organize and train farmers to make better use of their resources. USAID has also initiated infrastructure programs in Paktya. In the spring of 2009, the Tennessee Army National Guard Agribusiness Development Team (ADT) arrived in Paktya to address some of these problems. The team currently has approximately 35 ongoing projects, including building new greenhouses, rechanneling waterways for irrigation, and expanding the beekeeping industry.

Other Key Sectors

Agriculture serves as the foundation for most of the remainder of the economy. Difficult terrain and poor roads require that substantial resources be devoted to transportation, especially trucking. Butchers, blacksmiths, harness makers, and retailers selling basic house wares and farm implements are all staples of any town in Paktya.

Small operations quarrying lower-grade marble and mining chromite are the only exploitation of mineral resources in the province.

Additionally, licit and illicit trade across the border with Pakistan generates some income, although not on the scale seen in some other provinces. No significant manufacturing activity exists in the province.

International assistance provides the current boost to the economy. While compiling precise figures is difficult, the Commander's Emergency Response Program (CERP – military funding projects) alone provided more than $35 million to the economy in 2008 by building roads, schools, and other infrastructure projects, usually with local labor and, when possible, using labor-intensive methods. Indeed between 2007 and 2009, the PRT CERP budget for Paktya rose from around $8 million to $70 million.

INFRASTRUCTURE

Transportation

The road from Kabul to Gardez is the major economic artery for the province and remains the only road in good condition after repairs in 2008 by USAID. The road from Gardez to Khost is currently being repaired. The route from the border through northern Paktya is the shortest route from Pakistan to Kabul. The route from Khost through Gardez to Ghazni connects that fertile province to markets in the rest of Afghanistan, and, when improved, will allow farmers throughout southern Afghanistan to take their fruits and vegetables to market. Despite this strategic location, roads in Paktya have been undeveloped or neglected. In 2009, the PRT began work on an improved north-south road to connect Gardez to the northern districts it is supposed to govern. This road will also facilitate the movement of goods from farms in the north to market.

The Gardez airport has been reopened after being cleared of mines. However, there are no tower facilities and it is being used by coalition forces and NGO-contracted flights only after the military has secured the area.

Electricity

A small diesel power generator in Gardez provides limited power to government offices and the city center, but only for a few hours per day. While users are supposed to pay for usage, many subscribers ignore their bills while others illegally tap into the system. Some towns and villages have small private or communal hydroelectric generators but developing metering and payment schemes to make these power sources self-sustaining is a challenge in a country with little experience in such matters. The many mountain streams provide the potential for additional micro-hydro projects.

The Kajaki Dam in Helmand Province, currently being refurbished by USAID, may supply power to southern Paktya as early as mid-2010, if the currently planned transmission lines can be built and secured. Negotiations are also underway to import power from Pakistan for the northern half of the province. In the interim, solar-powered lights are increasingly in use throughout the province, small hydroelectric projects provide power to isolated local areas, and three hybrid power projects provide electricity to Zormat, Sayed Karam, and Mirzaka.

Telecommunications

There are no significant landline networks in Paktya but mobile phones have dramatically increased their coverage in recent years. Three cellular phone systems are currently active: the government-owned Afghan Wireless Communication Company (AWCC), Roshan Wireless, and Areeba. Gardez and the central valley enjoy full cell phone coverage, and there is also adequate coverage along the main roads (to Kabul, Zormat, and Khost). In the mountainous areas, service is limited but improving. Along the Pakistan border, many people buy phones with Pakistani service codes – as Afghan providers have not yet established service there. In some areas, cell towers are shut down during evening hours as part of agreements with insurgent forces.

The UN Refugee Agency, UNHCR, is one of many UN agencies which work alongside the military and PRTs. It works to provide schools, infrastructure, health services, and capacity building critical to boosting the provincial economy.

PHOTO BY TOM PRASTER

Chapter 5
International Organizations and Reconstruction Activities

As violence has increased in southern and eastern Afghanistan, many NGOs and International Organizations (IOs) have closed their offices or have lowered their profile and reconstruction activity has slowed. While this has occurred to some extent in Paktya, UNAMA and other organizations have maintained their presence, and the effects on economic development have been less than in other provinces where the NGOs and IOs left entirely.

PROVINCIAL RECONSTRUCTION TEAM (PRT)

As the site of the first Afghan PRT in early 2003, Paktya has seen the focus of US assistance change over time – from the initial urgent rush to dig wells and build schools and clinics, to a shift to larger, longer-term development projects and a focus on building indigenous human capacity. Currently there is a blend of heavy infrastructure projects, such as roads, and smaller schools, clinics, and water projects to meet the immediate needs of towns and villages. The ADT is co-located with the PRT and reports to brigade headquarters. It fills the gap the PRT left in the agriculture sector by the lack of any consistent, substantial agriculture assistance program.

Currently, the PRT consists of about 80 personnel, with the integrated command group consisting of the PRT commander and representatives from USAID, USDA, and the Department of State. Generally, PRTs focus on transportation, energy, education, health, and governance/rule of law. Roads are considered a basis for improvement across all sectors, and they are by far the most expensive projects. Road construction accounted for approximately 45 percent of CERP funds in 2008. The CERP allocation of approximately $35 million in 2008 approximately doubled in 2009, in line with the expected increase in CERP allocations to Afghanistan.

NATIONAL SOLIDARITY PROGRAM (NSP)

Paktya completed the first phase of its National Solidarity Program (NSP) in 2008. Two hundred seventy one projects, including roads, culverts, irrigation canals, construction and cleaning of *karezes*, drinking water wells and water reservoirs, solar and hydro power plants, mosques and other social centers, and literacy courses worth $2.6 million were completed in accordance with the mandates of CDCs. The NSP program is implemented nationally through the Ministry of Rural Rehabilitation and Development (MRRD), originally with World Bank funding. In Paktya, the NSP program provides a successful example of the central government responding to the priorities identified by individuals in the most remote corners of the province.

PROJECTS AND ACTIVITIES

Electricity

In the long-term, plans to provide Paktyans with a stable source of electricity are being made outside the province through the reconstruction of the Kajaki Dam in Helmand and negotiations to import electricity from other provinces or countries. The PRT has several CERP projects underway to provide more immediate solutions. A hydroelectric dam in Ahmad Abad will provide electricity to approximately 975 residential compounds. In Sayed Karam, a hybrid power plant – wind, solar, and diesel – will provide electricity to approximately 400 homes. Similar projects are underway in Zormat and Mirzaka. Micro-hydro projects for remote villages are being provided by USAID. These projects should be completed in 2010.

Transportation

Roads have a multitude of developmental impacts and are thus a priority. They provide improved access to hospitals and schools. For farmers, improved roads are seen as a way to break the cycle of subsistence farming, allowing them greater access to markets and opportunity to bring to market perishable fruits and vegetables which would otherwise be destroyed in transit on potholed dirt roads. For the consumer, the prices of products in markets are reduced as transport times, and thus costs, decrease. In addition to the social and economic benefits, these roads will also allow government officials and security forces to reach remote areas, significantly improving their ability to serve the people.

USAID is currently paving the Gardez-Khost road, which will help link the Paktya farmers to markets in the east. USAID began paving the Gardez-Ghazni road through Zormat in the spring of 2009. When completed, these two projects will link Khost to the Ring Road, the main highway connecting all the major cities of Afghanistan. The PRT received approval to use CERP funds to pave the road northeast from Gardez through Sayed Karam to Ahmed Khel. They are seeking to connect to spurs funded by the US Army and USAID running east through Dand Wa Patan to Pakistan and west to Logar (some of these will be paved, and others graveled). Other PRT plans include a Gardez-Sharan road, allowing farmers from Sharan, Paktika to move their goods to Kabul and Khost, and a road along the eastern border from Jani Khel to Waza Zadran.

Irrigation

Most of southern Paktya agriculture relies on irrigation systems, including the underground karez systems. The required maintenance to keep these systems viable has been neglected for 30 years. USDA and USAID have conducted irrigation projects, but not on a large scale. Unfortunately, the violence in Zormat has prevented any extensive work in the district, where it is needed the most.

Other Agriculture

USAID has provided veterinary training, agricultural business training, and training for women to grow kitchen gardens. It has introduced a Community Agriculture Development Program (CADP) to improve quality and to improve infrastructure. CADP projects include introducing better seed and orchard seedlings, and demonstration projects to store apples in cellars. Apple prices triple from harvest time through mid-winter, but without storage facilities, farmers have to sell their apples during the period of lowest prices.

Table 7: Number of Schools, Teachers, and Students in Paktya

NUMBER OF	SCHOOLS	STUDENTS			TEACHERS		
		MALE	FEMALE	TOTAL	MALE	FEMALE	TOTAL
Primary	117	15,662	7,296	22,958	917	10	927
Middle	58	19,759	8,277	28,036	564	19	583
High	46	47,677	5,522	53,199	1,010	69	1,07v9
Informal	121	1,047	2,566	3,613	97	24	121
Madrassas	16	1,602	0	1,602	48	0	48
TOTAL	358	85,747	23,661	109,408	2,636	122	2,758

The addition of a 60-soldier ADT from the Tennessee Army National Guard should dramatically increase the number of agricultural projects (especially as it has its own budget). Indeed the ADT has initiated sustainability schemes to ensure continued development among Afghans. These projects include furniture-manufacturing training courses, basic animal husbandry courses, beehive construction courses, para-veterinary training programs, and training on poultry, sheep, and goat husbandry for disadvantaged women and youth.

Education

Less than 25 percent of men and 10 percent of women in Paktya are literate, but most desire to see their children perform better. The building and equipping of schools by the PRT, USAID, UNHCR, and others is regularly praised by officials and members of the public, and a desire for more schools is still part of every development plan. Some parents in this conservative area want to see their children receive a religious education and send their sons to madrassas, but the majority are happy with or anxious for government schools.

There are 117 primary, 58 middle, and 46 high schools in Paktya. There also 121 "community-based home schools" run by International Rescue Committee (IRC). The home schools provide at least some access to education in areas where the government has yet to establish formal schools. Although theoretically these schools are based in private homes, in most cases the local mosques are used.

Elementary school enrollment in Paktya in 2003 was 65 percent (74 percent for boys, 55 percent for girls), significantly higher than the national average of 37 percent. This figure is significantly higher because 85 percent of boys who did not attend school in 2003 did so because a school was either non-existent or too far away. The PRT and USAID, among others, have built a substantial number of schools since then. Nevertheless, there is still a lack of buildings and supplies, as well as a dearth of qualified teachers.

The university in Gardez, which has been operating since 2006 with assistance from CERP funds, is admitting 176 students per year for classes in education and agriculture. The District Director of Education plans to expand the program to engineering and medicine in the near future.

USAID has built 29 schools in Paktya, and provided textbooks through the USAID national education program.

Healthcare

The Ministry of Health supports three different levels of health facilities for the country: hospitals, comprehensive health clinics, and basic health clinics. In 2009, Paktya had four hospitals (Gardez, Chamkani, Zazi, and Zormat), at least 16 comprehensive clinics, at least 22 basic health clinics, and a regional ANSF hospital which treats civilians when space permits.

USAID has constructed or refurbished over 40 medical facilities in Paktya, and trained 200 doctors and midwives. They are currently supporting a number of national programs to develop infrastructure, educate the public, assist private sector health providers, and expand health services. In August 2009, USAID signed an $800,000 grant agreement with the Afghanistan Urban Water Supply and Sanitation Corporation to support water infrastructure rehabilitation, equipment purchase, and training for the municipal water departments of Gardez and three other cities. Residents will enjoy improved access to clean water and sanitation services, as well as a more sustainable water supply, to strengthen public health and hygiene.

Governance

Historically, USAID has built or refurbished government buildings. A change in emphasis in the last few years has been the Local Government and Community Development program (LGCD), which seeks to provide provincial and district government with the infrastructure and training they require. Current activities include training for the provincial council, sub-governors, and the provincial development committee.

Table 8: Active Assistance Organizations

ACRONYM	FULL NAME	ACTIVITIES
DAI	Development Alternatives, Inc.	Implementing Partner for USAID; Local Government
DRAA	Development and Rehabilitation Agency for Afghanistan	Water and Sanitation
GTZ	Gesellschaft fur Technische Zusammenarbeit	Education
Ibn-Sina	N/A	Health
IRC	International Rescue Committee	Education, Water, and Sanitation
NEEP	National Emergency Employment Program	UNOPS implementing partner cash-for-work for widows, disabled, etc.

INTERNATIONAL ORGANIZATIONS AND THE UNITED NATIONS

The UN Assistance Mission Afghanistan (UNAMA) has maintained its South East Region (SER) office in Gardez since 2002. UNAMA SER is a political mission, and not an assistance or donor organization. Because it has a relatively large local staff and lower turnover of international staff, it is arguably the most knowledgeable organization in the province regarding the state of governance, economy, and social programs. Most NGOs in the area coordinate with, or at least inform, UNAMA of their activities. One of UNAMA's mandates is a requirement to assist in development coordination and promote aid effectiveness. There are several additional UN family members who have been active in Paktya (see Table 8).

Table 9: UN Agency Activities

ACRONYM	FULL NAME	MAIN ACTIVITIES
UNDP-ANBP	UN Development Program - Afghanistan's New Beginning Program	Disarmament of Illegally Armed Groups, Ammunitions - Security
UNDP-AIMS	UN Development Program - Afghanistan Information Management Services	Capacity Building working with the PRT
UNHCR	UN High Commissioner for Refugees	Infrastructure, health services, capacity building, water and sanitation
WHO	World Health Organization	NIDs (Health)
FAO	Food and Agriculture Organization	Food and forestry programs
IOM	International Organization for Migration	Afghan civil assistance; support to provincial government; assistance to Afghan families deported from Iran Water and Sanitation
UNDP-NABDP	National Area-Based Development Program	Karez and canal cleaning; intake construction for agriculture industry; digging wells; canal rehabilitation; road construction; support to water supply infrastructure
WFP	World Food Program	Education, Cleaning and rehabilitating of roads, canals and karez, food distribution projects, water and sanitation
UNICEF	UN Children's Fund	Provide schools with learning and teaching materials, furniture, teacher training, medication, water, and sanitation
UNOPS	UN Office for Project Services	Road Construction

Television stations are available in Paktya for those who can afford a television set, but the lack of electricity and low literacy rates have made radio stations and bazaar gossip the most popular sources of local and national news.

PHOTO BY TOM PRASTER

Chapter 6
Information and Influence

The ability of the electronic news media to directly influence the attitudes of Paktyans is limited by the lack of electricity for televisions, the limited reach of radio transmissions, and the natural Pashtun suspicion of strangers. Similarly, the print media is hindered by low levels of literacy and difficulties of distribution. However, these sources are not irrelevant; they serve primarily as a source for the most common method of spreading news: word of mouth. A report of an incident on the radio or television may be picked up and spread by mullahs in their Friday sermons, by villagers sitting under a tree drinking chai, or by young people on their cell phones. The constant retelling may mutate the story beyond recognition, but the final fantastic version will soon be more accepted than the original because it is heard from a friend or neighbor.

As difficult as it is to promulgate news in Paktya, it is equally difficult to learn what people are thinking. Pashtuns are reluctant to believe a stranger and are similarly reluctant to share their true beliefs and allegiances. After enduring many covert wars in recent centuries, many believe that the wisest approach is to watch, wait, and avoid commitment to either side. The best way to elicit genuine opinions from Paktyans is to sit down with them for long sessions of tea and relaxed conversation. Locals sometimes do not reveal their real feelings about a topic for hours, days, or months, if ever.

MEDIA

Radio

Radio is the most pervasive medium in Paktya. It is not only cheap, but a majority of people can receive at least a few stations, even if only on crank-powered radios. The BBC's Pashto service is likely the most influential source for national and international news. **Gardez Radio** is the government-owned station, broadcasting two hours in the morning and two hours in the evening. Two private radio stations, **Arman** and **Paktya Ghag** broadcast 12 hours per day. Music dominates most stations' lineups, but some also host call-in shows, information programs, and news bulletins. Rigorous public discourse and challenging journalism are almost non-existent on radio or television. Four "Radio-in-a-Box" (RIAB) stations had been established in the province by the spring of 2009. Equipment and technical assistance is provided by the US military, and some public information announcements are broadcast, but the majority of the programming and broadcasting is done by locals.

Television

Five television stations are available in Gardez using just a basic antenna. The newest is **Shamshad TV**, the first pure Pashto-language station in the country. Shamshad was founded in 2006 as a satellite station, but a new ground transmitter in Kabul, funded by USAID, makes it available with a basic antenna. Government-funded **Gardez TV** broadcasts programs directly from Kabul TV for five hours every day. Its programming includes a local news bulletin in both Pashto and Dari, as well as features on the main activities in the province. Three private stations, **Ariana**, **Tolo** and **Lemar**, rebroadcast their national programs for reception in Paktya offering a mix of entertainment and informational programming. Broadcasts are limited to four or five hours per day.

Cable and satellite television are available to those who can afford them, but their limited availability makes them less influential than radio or broadcast television.

Newspapers, Magazines, and the Internet

Written media has limited appeal in Paktya because less than 25 percent of males and 10 percent of females are literate. Nevertheless, there are two weeklies in the province, both based in Gardez. *Waranga* is government-funded, but suffered from lack of funding for several years. It is now regularly available. *The Paktya Ghag* (Voice of Paktya) is a private magazine. Monthly and bi-monthly magazines include *Suleman Ghar, Zarka, Aryoub, Wawra,* and *Nakhtar.* They focus on political, social, and cultural issues as well as literature and education.

There are internet cafes in Gardez, but so few people use the internet that it is not even a significant source of word-of-mouth news.

MOSQUES

As widespread as radio and television have become, the mullahs still have a greater influence over the population through their weekly Friday sermons which penetrate even into the remotest villages. More importantly, no radio or television personality has the moral authority and trust of the population that is enjoyed by the local mullah. It is essential to be aware of what is being said in the mosques and to work towards ensuring that religious leaders understand the goals of the international community in Afghanistan.

The mountains of Paktya are home to illegal loggers, smugglers, bandits, and insurgents. Since 2006, both the Haqqani Network and Hezb-e Islami Gulbuddin (HIG) have expanded their operations in the province.

PHOTO BY TOM PRASTER

Chapter 7
The Big Issues

SECURITY AND EXTENDING THE REACH OF THE GOVERNMENT

After 30 years of unrest, the overwhelming majority of the population in Paktya still desires an end to the violence. However, eight years after the Bonn meeting which established the Afghan Interim Authority, people are no longer optimistic that the government can deliver that result. Paktyans expected Karzai to unite the Pashtun nation and, together with coalition forces, usher in a new era of peace and prosperity. Among the most common complaints one hears in the province is that Karzai has allowed Northern Alliance strongmen to hold too much power in the central government and that Tajik influence in the security forces, especially in the NDS, has put Pashtuns in an alarmingly weak position.

It is beyond the scope of this handbook to analyze the course Karzai has taken in the interests of uniting and pacifying all of Afghanistan. It is, however, clear that the Paktyans' loss of confidence in Kabul, for both this reason and for the perceived incompetence and corruption of the central government, has cost Karzai his base in the Pashtun heart-land, leaving the door open for the Haqqani Network, HIG, and Taliban forces to re-enter an area where they had been almost extinguished.

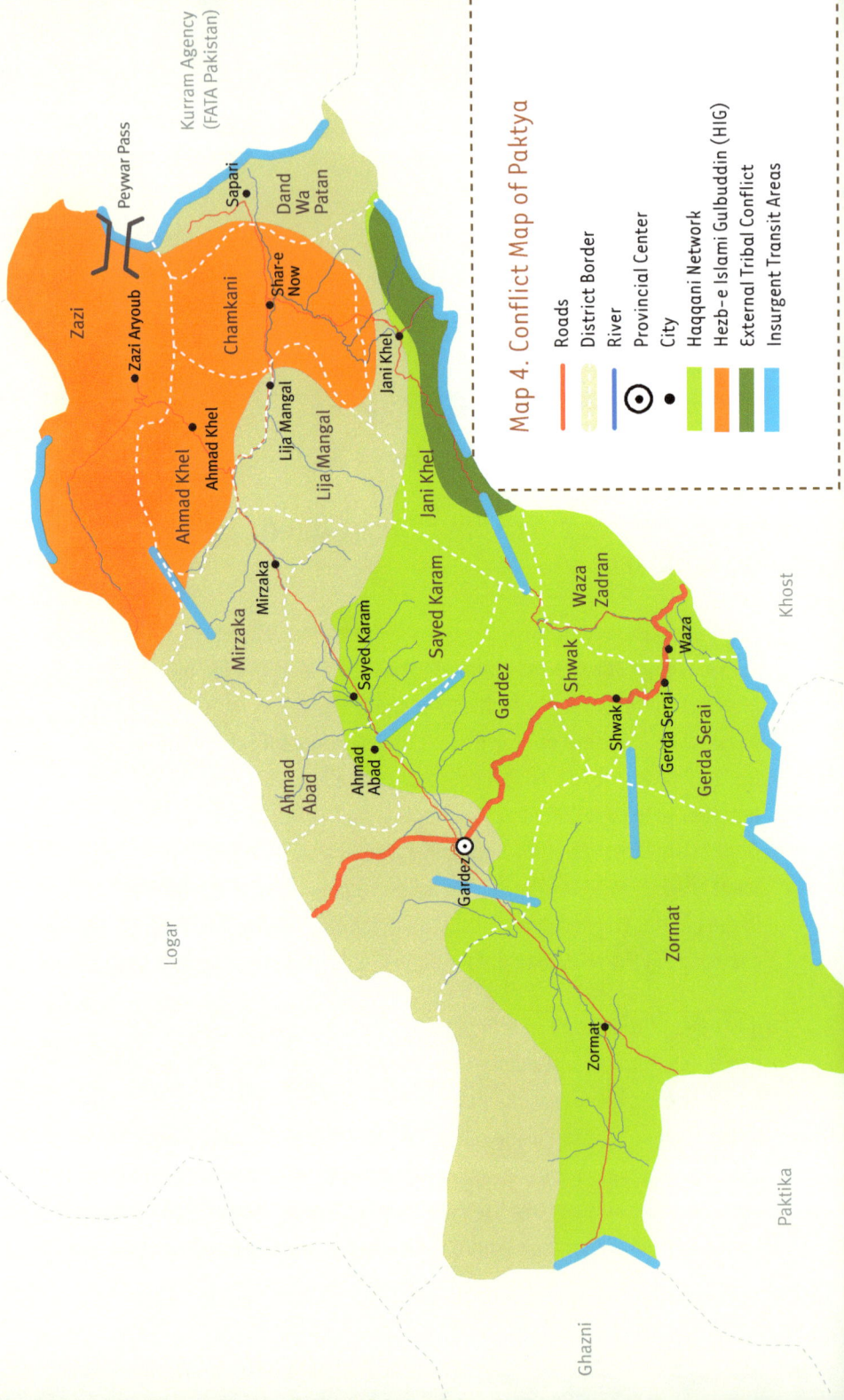

Map 4. Conflict Map of Paktya

Legend:

- Roads
- District Border
- River
- Provincial Center
- City
- Haqqani Network
- Hezb-e Islami Gulbuddin (HIG)
- External Tribal Conflict
- Insurgent Transit Areas

Kurram Agency (FATA Pakistan)

Peywar Pass

Zazi

Zazi Aryoub

Sapari

Dand Wa Patan

Chamkani

Shar-e Now

Jani Khel

Ahmad Khel

Lija Mangal

Lija Mangal

Jani Khel

Mirzaka

Mirzaka

Sayed Karam

Sayed Karam

Waza Zadran

Shwak

Waza

Gardez

Shwak

Gerda Serai

Gerda Serai

Ahmad Abad

Ahmad Abad

Gardez

Zormat

Zormat

Logar

Khost

Paktika

Ghazni

In addition to the political opening, the insurgent groups have taken advantage of the weakness of coalition partners and ANSF in the region. While Paktya was one of the earliest provinces to receive an ANA deployment (April 2003) and hosts the 203rd Corps headquarters, Afghan and ISAF forces alike have been stretched thin dealing with deteriorating situations in Helmand, Kandahar, Paktika, and Nuristan. ANP and ANBP in Paktya have rarely been staffed at more than 50 percent of authorized strength. While corruption and desertion have plagued those services nationwide, constant turmoil in provincial leadership has intensified their deficiencies in Paktya. Local commanders who were already committed to the insurgency or leaning in that direction refused to participate in the Disarming of Illegally Armed Groups (DIAG) program, and the government was unable to force compliance with the program.

While the Haqqani Network never abandoned its base in Shah-i Kot Valley in Zormat, in earlier years most of its operations were small and conducted across the border. However, the number of security incidents increased dramatically in 2005 and 2006, and Governor Tanaiwal sanctioned the formation of *arbakai* to help offset the ineffective ANSF. Unfortunately, Taniwal was assassinated by a Haqqani suicide bomber in September of 2006. Since then, the Haqqani Network has begun operating outside Zadran areas and has strengthened its base in Gerda Serai, Haqqani's birthplace.

Hezb-e Islami Gulbuddin (HIG) seems to be following a similar trajectory to the Haqqani Network. While it was formerly limited to districts in Khost along the Pakistan border and made occasional forays in the Zazi and Chamkhani areas, by 2008 it had apparently established a more permanent presence in those districts and was expanding its activities to Lija Mangal and Sayed Karam. The more it is able to assert control in the north, the easier it is for insurgent groups to transit Paktya to Logar, a staging area for attacks on Kabul.

Saifur Rehman Mansoor continues to operate with relative impunity in Zormat. He probably has the closest ties to the Afghan Taliban leadership located in Pakistan. Efforts to root out his operatives have, unfortunately, often angered the local population.

However, more ANA and ANP are helping to improve the situation. A scheduled increase of coalition forces may also encourage progress.

ECONOMIC DEVELOPMENT

Paktya has been the recipient of considerable foreign assistance, though its residents and elders frequently, and correctly, point out that development funds spent in the province have been far outpaced by those in neighboring provinces, particularly Khost. But there have been clear improvements in education, health, transportation, and sanitation in Paktya. More important than the relative measures is the low baseline from which the province started, and the high expectations of the population who feel things should be better. Some responsibility must also go to the international community as not all of the projects it has sponsored have turned out well. Deficiencies in the international community's contracting have led to charges of corruption or incompetence, and lapses in quality control have resulted in projects collapsing before they are a year old. The number of such incidents may be exaggerated, but enough have occurred to undermine faith in the ability of the government and the international community to improve Paktyans' lives.

Another deficiency of development assistance has been in the lack of attention paid to agriculture. While the need for schools and clinics is real and visible to outsiders, the problems with agriculture are not as evident to non-agricultural professionals and have not caught the attention of many donors. The deployment of a single USDA officer at the PRT and a small USAID Community Development agriculture office working from the FOB in Gardez has been a band-aid on a gaping wound. It is agriculture that either directly or indirectly provides the livelihood for most of the people in the province. This is especially true in Zormat, the most populous and, in the past, most agriculturally productive district in the province. The deployment of an Agribusiness Development Team (ADT) is a step in the right direction. *(Please see chapter 6 for a full description of ADT activities.)*

Blacksmiths like this man are a staple of towns in Paktya, making farm instruments which are critical for the 45% of the population which engages in farming.

PHOTO BY TOM PRASTER

APPENDICES

TIMELINE OF EVENTS

2001: Civil war breaks out between tribal elder Pacha Khan Zadran and the Tajik minority based out of Gardez.

2002: Pacha Khan Zadran flees Gardez, shelling the city in the process. Operation Anaconda, coalition forces battle al-Qaeda and Taliban fighters in Shah-i Kot Valley, Zormat district.

2003: First PRT established near Gardez.

2004: Pacha Khan Zadran is captured in Pakistan and extradited to Kabul. There, he makes peace with President Karzai.

2006: Governor Taniwal killed in a suicide attack outside his office, replaced by Rahmatullah Rahmat.

2008: Governor Rahmat replaced by Juma Khan Hamdard.

2009: Suicide bombers attack government buildings in Gardez.

March 1, 2010: Paktya's NDS arrest three provincial judges for soliciting bribes from released prisoners; one was employed in security affairs.

COMMON COMPLIMENTS REGARDING THE US MILITARY IN SOUTHEASTERN AFGHANISTAN

- Afghans compliment the work ethic of US forces and say it drives them to work harder for themselves.

- Afghans are happy with projects such as roads that improve their lives after decades of war.

- Other foreign armies have come to conquer; the US military has come to help Afghans.

- Afghans respect the US forces for leaving their families to come and help them.

COMMON COMPLAINTS REGARDING THE US MILITARY IN SOUTHEASTERN AFGHANISTAN

- Afghans claim that US forces have inflicted excessive civilian casualties while taking out few insurgent leaders.

- Afghans complain that the US forces raid their houses at night without cause or government support. Afghans believe US forces use informers for their intelligence gathering and assistance project priorities who are not being honest. Most of these people have their own agendas and manipulate the truth.

- Afghans say US forces and USAID pay too much for their projects, sometimes triple what Afghans would pay, and the quality is often poor. Afghans believe US forces are being manipulated by or are supporting the corrupt politicians who are behind the dishonest contractors.

- Afghans lament that coalition forces and other foreign personnel do not know or understand more about the local people and what is going on among them.

DAY IN THE LIFE OF A RURAL PAKTYAN

The schedule of daily life in rural Paktya depends on the season. Country people rise before dawn to offer the first of their five daily prayers. Women build a fire over which they cook flat loaves of bread in the *tandoor*, a stone oven. Breakfast typically consists of bread mashed in milk, or bread with cheese or curds, washed down with milk tea. During the spring and summer growing season, the women set out to the fields to spend their day weeding, fertilizing, and irrigating. Before noon they pause to eat a small snack of bread and say their midday prayers before returning to their arduous agricultural work. At dusk they return home to cook dinner, which usually consists of more bread, different vegetables based on the season, and yogurt milk. In the spring wild greens supplement the meal; later in the season, beans, peas, and squash are also eaten.

Men are in charge of the livestock, which many families own for milk. The cows feed off the corn and wheat stalks after harvest, and grasses in mountain pastures. During the summer months, men spend their days in the pastures, herding the goats on their daily grazing rounds and producing the various types of cheese and curds derived from the animals' milk. Several men will pool their livestock and manpower resources, taking turns with the chores.

During the fall, women spend their days gathering firewood for the next season's heating and cooking. In winter months, after harvesting and settling in, daily life slows. Women tend to household chores; men hang out around the mosque or with friends, playing games or just talking about everyday events. Children will attend school and assist with household chores.

FURTHER READING AND SOURCES

Books

- NATO, *ISAF PRT Handbook*, 3rd Ed. February 2007.

- Sarah Chayes, *The Punishment of Virtue: Inside Afghanistan After the Taliban*, New York: Penguin Press, 2006.

- Steve Coll, *Ghost Wars: The Secret History of the CIA, Afghanistan, and Bin Laden, From the Soviet Invasion to September 10, 2001*, New York: Penguin Press, 2004.

- Louis Dupree, *Afghanistan*, Princeton: Princeton University Press, 1979.

- Edward R. Girardet, *Afghanistan: The Soviet War*. New Delhi, India: Selectbook Service Syndicate, 1985.

- Edward Girardet and Jonathan Walter, *Afghanistan: Essential Field Guides to Humanitarian and Conflict Zones*, CROSSLINES Publication Ltd, 1998 and 2004. *www.crosslinesguides.com*

- Larry Goodson, *Afghanistan's Endless War: State Failure, Regional Politics, and the Rise of the Taliban,* Seattle: University of Washington Press, 2001.

- Michael Griffin, *Reaping the Whirlwind*: *The Taliban Movement in Afghanistan*, London: Pluto Press, 2001.

- Ben Macintyre, *The Man Who Would Be King: The First American in Afghanistan*, New York: Farrar, Straus and Giroux, 2005.

- Greg Mortenson, *Three Cups of Tea: One Man's Mission to Promote Peace ... One School at a Time*, New York: Penguin Books, 2006. (excellent understanding of how to succeed with the people and culture)

- Sean Naylor, *Not a Good Day to Die: The Untold Story of Operation Anaconda*, London: Penquin/Michael Joseph, 2005.

- Ahmed Rashid, *Descent into Chaos: The United States and the Future of Nation Building in Afghanistan, Pakistan, and Central Asia*, New York: Viking Press, 2008.

- Ahmed Rashid, *Taliban: Militant Islam, Oil and Fundamentalism in Central Asia*, New Haven: Yale University Press, 2000.

- Barnett Rubin, *The Fragmentation of Afghanistan*, New Haven: Yale University Press, 2001.

Articles

- Hamed Karzai, *The Afghanistan National Development Strategy*, 2006, *www.reliefweb.int/rw/RWFiles2006.nsf/ dbc12f058effd2dac125749600457fd4/c125723c004042d7c12573aa00 474d8b/$FILE/unama-afg-30jan2.pdf*

- Raphy Favre, *Potential Analysis of the Eastern Region and Nangarhar Province and Implication in Programming,* September 2005, *http://aizon.org/Nangarhar%20Potential%20Analysis.pdf*

- G.H. Orris and J.D. Bliss (eds), *Mines and Mineral Occurrences of Afghanistan,* open-file report 02-110, U S .Geological Survey, US Department of the Interior, 2002.

- Barnett Rubin, "Afghanistan's Uncertain Transition from Turmoil to Normalcy," *Council Special Report*, No. 12, March 2007.

- Wilder, Andrew. "Cops or Robbers: The Struggle to Reform the Afghan National Police," *Afghan Research and Evaluation Unit*, July 2007, *www.areu.org.af/index php?option=com_docman&task=doc_download&gid=523*

Web Sites

- Afghanistan Research and Evaluation Unit (publishes the *Afghanistan A to Z guide*), *www.areu.org.af/index. php?option=com_frontpage&Itemid=25*

- Afghanistan Information Management Services, *www.aims.org.af*

- Afghanistan Online (Links to Official IRA and embassy websites), *www afghan-web.com/politics*

- Naval Postgraduate School Program for Culture and Conflict Studies, *www nps.edu/Programs/CCS/index html*

- USAID, *www.usaid.gov/locations/asia/countries/afghanistan*

www.ingramcontent.com/pod-product-compliance
Lightning Source LLC
Chambersburg PA
CBHW040128270326
41927CB00001B/25